MUSICIANS INSTITUTE

PRIVATE LESSONS

Harmony Vocals

by Mike Campbell
& Tracee Lewis

MW00612379

ISBN 0-7935-8878-2

HAL•LEONARD®
CORPORATION

7777 W. BLUEMOUND RD. P.O. BOX 13819 MILWAUKEE, WI 53213

Copyright © 2001 by HAL LEONARD CORPORATION
International Copyright Secured   All Rights Reserved

Visit Hal Leonard Online at
www.halleonard.com

Preface

This is a book for singers of all ages—in particular, it's for anyone who has ever listened to a vocal group or background vocal and said, "Wow... I love that sound!" *Harmony Vocals* covers basic ear training and sightsinging, harmony and theory from unison lines to four-part harmony, and essential stage and studio techniques, all pulled together into a user-friendly format. The companion CD allows you to listen, learn, and participate in singing harmonies. It's our hope that *Harmony Vocals* will make learning to sing harmonies a reality for even the most inexperienced vocalist.

—*Mike Campbell & Tracee Lewis Meyn*

Acknowledgments

From Mike Campbell

Just a few words to say "Thank you" to Tracee Lewis Meyn for her help and friendship through seven wonderful years at Musicians Institute. She was my "right hand" when I was hired to head the vocal department at MI. This book would not have happened if Tracee hadn't agreed to be my partner in this project. Even though she has moved to Norway, she is always in my heart and thoughts.

The faculty at MI has been like a family to me. Les Coulter, Jami Lula, Dena Murray, "Masta" Edwards, Ken Stacey, Carol Rogers, Claudia Neault, Coreen Sheehan, Julie Kelly, Cathy Segal Garcia, Tomie Reeves, Tina von Busek, and Joey Barclay have been especially inspirational friends and colleagues. A more passionate and caring group of teachers is unimaginable. They've inspired me to be a better teacher, and it's been a privilege to work with them over the years.

A very special thank you to Jeanette Mishler. A wonderful engineer, terrific teacher, total madman at the gym, and constant joy to be around.

From Tracee Lewis Meyn

I would like to thank God that we finished this book, which has seen and lived through four computers, a marriage, a move to Norway, a kid going to college, and many cozy dinners at the Campbells. Thank you Elaine Campbell, my husband Knut, and Hal Leonard Corporation for your patience, Henry Brewer for making our lives so very easy, Jeanette Mishler for working miracles, and most of all Mike Campbell for giving me the opportunity to share this experience with him. What a blast!

Contents

1 GETTING STARTED

et's start with the essentials: scales, intervals, and chords—and how to sing them. Singers sometimes feel they "don't need to know this stuff." After all, they just open their mouths, and it's all there, right? Well maybe for some people, but as a rule, most vocalists need at least a little training. Even if you have a perfect voice and a wonderful ear, it always helps to know a little about what you're doing.

There are many aspects to singing, especially if you're going to sing backing vocals. You never know when someone will throw a chart in front of you and ask, "Do you read?" or say, "Oh, just make up some parts, will ya?" (We vocalists typically want to respond, "Okay, just give me some vocal arranger credit, will ya?")

As a singer, it's good for you to at least know the basics. What's a key signature? What's a staff? What are all those little black dots? For some of you this may be old news, but for those of you just beginning, this is an introduction into the musician's world, of which you are a part. Don't just think of yourself as a "singer"; think of yourself as a musician with the most natural and beautiful instrument of all, the voice. When you're trying to communicate with other musicians, or they with you, knowing the basics of harmony and theory, being able to read a little, and having some idea of what is going on around you can help tremendously.

How to Read Music

One reason music is known as a "universal language" is that is has a written notation system all its own. It's full of all types of symbols and figures you may never have seen before—or that you may have seen but didn't know what the heck they were.

Staff & Clef

Music is written on a series of lines and spaces called a *staff*. To capture the full range of pitches available, two staves are typically used—one with a *treble clef* (or "G clef"), the other with a *bass clef* (or "F clef").

Treble clef is used for music and voices in the high registers—female voice, male tenor voice, guitar, right hand of the piano. Bass clef is used for music in the low registers—male bass voice, left hand of the piano.

Notes

Names of the notes follow the first seven letters of the alphabet—A, B, C, D, E, F, and G. A quick way to learn the notes on each staff is to break them down by lines and spaces. In treble clef, the lines of the staff, from bottom to top, are **E–G–B–D–F**. The spaces are **F–A–C–E**.

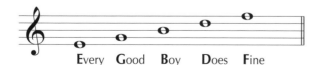

Every Good Boy Does Fine

F   A   C   E

In bass clef, the lines of the staff are **G–B–D–F–A**. The spaces are **A–C–E–G**.

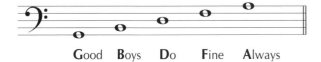

Good   Boys   Do   Fine   Always

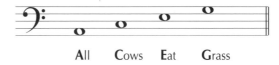

All   Cows   Eat   Grass

When the two clefs are combined, they form what is called a *grand staff*. Notice that notes can extend above and below the staff, with the use of ledger lines. In between the two staves is "middle C," a common reference note on the piano.

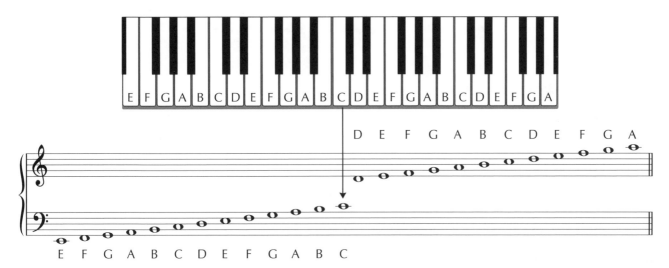

Half Steps & Whole Steps

Half steps and whole steps are a way of measuring the distance, or interval, between two notes. The shortest possible distance between two notes on a piano is a *half step*. Two half steps equal one *whole step*.

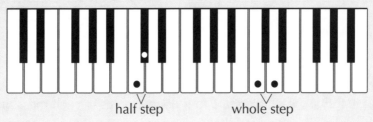

half step   whole step

Sharps & Flats

The notes A, B, C, D, E, F, and G are sometimes called "natural" notes; they correspond to the white keys on a piano. But what about the black keys, i.e., the notes in between? These are notated with sharps and flats.

Sharp (♯)
Raises a note a half step

Flat (♭)
Lowers a note a half step

Natural (♮)
Cancels a previous sharp or flat

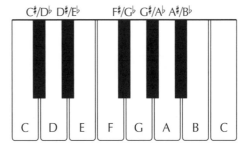

Notice that any black note can be spelled as a sharp or a flat, depending on the direction from which it's approached. Whether you use sharps or flats depends on the key of the song (more about that later). The technical term for two note names with the same pitch (e.g., C♯ and D♭) is *enharmonic equivalents*.

Note Durations

Every note has a duration or time value. This is felt in relation to the pulse or beat of the music. These basic note values also relate to each other proportionally:

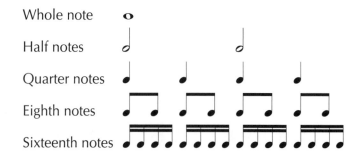

Time Signatures

Every measure (or "bar") of music has a certain number of beats in it. A *time signature* is a set of numbers—it looks like a fraction—that appears at the beginning of a piece of music. The top number tells you the number of beats in each measure, and the bottom number tells you what type of note value receives a beat, or count.

For example, in 4/4 time, the top number tells us there are four (4) beats in a measure, while the bottom number tells us that the quarter note (1/4) gets the count. In 3/4 time, there are three (3) beats in each measure, and the quarter note (1/4) gets the count. In 6/8 time, there are six (6) beats in a measure, and the eighth note (1/8) gets the count. In 12/8, there are twelve (12) beats in each measure, and the eighth note (1/8) gets the count.

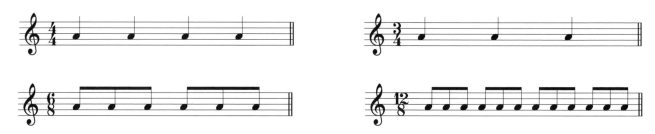

Subdiving the Beat

If the time signature is 4/4, that means there are four quarter notes in each measure and the quarter note gets the count. You can subdivide these four beats in any way you choose. Four quarter notes could be subdivided into 8 eighth notes or 16 sixteenth notes, for example.

count: 1   2   3   4   1 & 2 & 3 & 4 &   1 e & a 2 e & a 3 e & a 4 e & a

Rests

Rests are like notes, in time value, except they indicate silence instead of sound.

Whole rest	Half rest	Quarter rest	Eighth rest	Sixteenth rest

Ties & Dots

A *tie* is a curved line connecting two notes of the same pitch. You sing the first note of a tie and hold it for the duration of the combined note values. You must be able to tell the difference between a tie and a slur. Both are curved lines that go from one note to another, but a tie will only go to a note of the same pitch, while a *slur* tells you to slide from one pitch to another.

The *dot* is a device used to increase a note by half its own value. For example, a dotted quarter note equals a quarter note plus an eighth note. A dotted half note equals a half note plus a quarter note.

Scales

There are many types of scales—diatonic, pentatonic, blues, half-diminished, etc.—but for now, we'll concentrate on the most basic: major and minor. As a singer, these are the scales you'll most likely use when doing exercises, singing down a chart, or harmonizing a song. And knowing these basic scales can help you when practicing—you can use them to help warm up your voice, to work on your range, etc. Let's dive in, so you can learn how to identify them.

The Major Scale

You've heard singers, at least in the movies, singing "do-re-mi-fa-so-la-ti-do," right? Well, that's a major scale. A major scale consists of eight (8) notes. The starting note is called the *tonic*. It's the note from which the scale takes its name. The remaining notes follow a distinctive sequence of whole and half steps, which gives the scale its quality. The formula for a major scale is:

whole–whole–half–whole–whole–whole–half

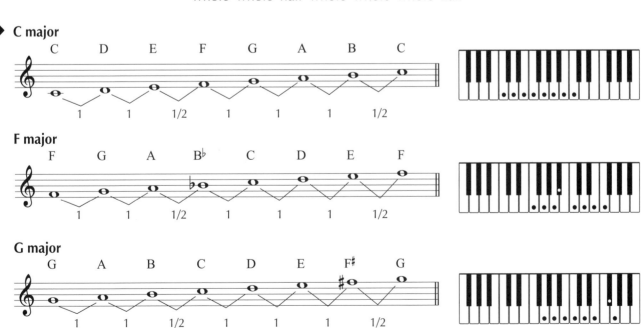

All major scales are built the same. The easiest way to remember this pattern is to notice where the half steps are located: between the 3rd and 4th steps and the 7th and 8th steps.

Key Signatures–Major

All written music and scales have key signatures. The key signature tells you what key the song or scale is in by telling you what notes to play or sing natural, sharp, or flat. It appears following the clef sign. The sharps and flats of the key signature are there to maintain the whole/half step relationships in the scale.

Knowing all of the key signatures is extremely important if you plan on doing commercial work or any other job where you have to sightsing. Not everything is written in the key of C! (Quick shortcut: To identify a key with sharps, move one half step up from the last sharp in the key signature; that's the name of the key. To identify a key with flats, name the second-to-last flat in the signature; that's the key's name.)

Minor Scales

Every major scale has a *relative minor scale*. It's called "relative" minor because it's comprised of the same notes as the major scale, just played in a different order. For example, the relative minor for the key of C is A minor (see below). Minor scales have a different, darker sound than major scales. You might think of the sound as being sadder. Another name for this scale is the *natural minor scale*. The formula is whole–half–whole–whole–half–whole–whole.

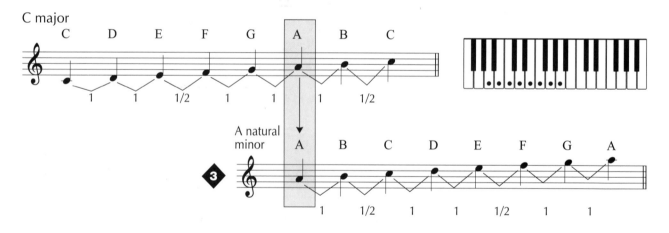

Notice the difference in quality? It's the 3rd, 6th, and 7th degrees of the scale that account for this difference; compared to the major scale, these notes are each a half step lower. In fact, in traditional sightsinging, the syllables used for these degrees are changed to reflect this:

			major								natural minor					
1	2	3	4	5	6	7	8		1	2	♭3	4	5	♭6	♭7	8
do	re	mi	fa	so	la	ti	do		do	re	me	fa	so	le	te	do

For various reasons, the natural minor scale is often altered, creating other minor scales. The third degree (♭3) never changes—it's the defining note of any minor scale—but the 6th and 7th degrees do. The *harmonic minor scale*, for example, shares the same notes as natural minor, but the 7th degree of the scale is raised:

3 A harmonic minor

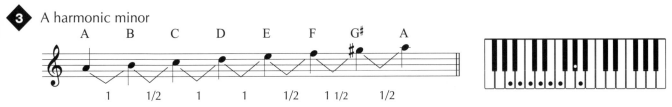

The *melodic minor scale* is a little different. The 6th and 7th degrees are raised one half step ascending. Descending, the notes are lowered, making them the same as the natural minor scale.

5 A melodic minor (ascending)

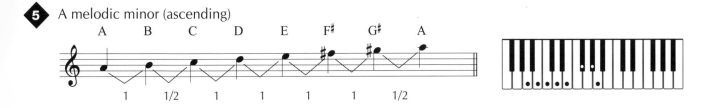

Key Signatures–Minor

Minor scales use the same key signatures as their relative major counterparts. A minor, for example, uses the same key signature as its relative, C major (no sharps or flats); E minor uses the same key signature as its relative, G major (one sharp); and so on.

NOTE: If the minor scale is altered—à la harmonic or melodic minor—those alterations appear in the music, not in the key signature.

The Chromatic Scale

The chromatic scale is unrelated to the major and minor scales—it doesn't have a tonic or key center—and simply consists of every possible note of the keyboard in successive half steps. It's a good warm-up or technical exercise.

6 Chromatic scale

Four-Note Fragments (Singing with Numbers)

Here we have an exercise in major and minor, using numbers only. This will strengthen your sense of key, and of major and minor. Play these on the piano—or listen to the CD—until you can start to sing them without help. That's the goal of this section: to be able to "hear" the melodies and sing them. You can start in the key of C, but also try different keys.

C major

do re mi fa so la ti do

1 2 3 4 5 6 7 8

C minor

do re me fa so le te do

1 2 ♭3 4 5 ♭6 ♭7 8

When singing the minor fragments, observe the flats (♭3, ♭6, and ♭7), but don't sing them. That is, flat the pitch, but pronounce only the numbers ("three," "six," and "seven").

7 MAJOR

1. 1–2–3–4	11. 1–2–4–2	21. 1–7–6–5
2. 5–6–7–8	12. 1–3–4–3	22. 2–4–6–8
3. 1–2–3–2	13. 1–5–3–5	23. 2–3–4–5
4. 1–3–2–3	14. 1–5–2–1	24. 2–5–3–6
5. 1–4–3–2	15. 1–6–5–4	25. 2–1–7–8
6. 1–3–4–5	16. 1–3–5–6	26. 3–6–2–5
7. 1–4–3–4	17. 1–6–5–6	27. 4–2–3–1
8. 1–5–4–3	18. 1–6–7–8	28. 5–7–8–1
9. 1–3–5–1	19. 1–7–8–7	29. 6–4–2–1
10. 1–5–3–1	20. 1–7–5–3	30. 7–8–3–1

8 MINOR

1. 1–♭3–2–1	11. 1–5–♭3–4	21. 1–♭7–4–♭3
2. 1–♭3–4–5	12. 1–4–♭3–2	22. 2–♭3–♭6–8
3. 1–♭3–♭6–♭7	13. 1–♭7–♭6–♭3	23. 2–5–♭3–♭6
4. 1–♭3–5–♭3	14. 1–♭6–5–4	24. 2–4–♭6–♭7
5. 1–5–♭3–2	15. 1–♭3–♭7–8	25. 2–1–♭6–5
6. 1–♭6–5–♭3	16. 1–♭3–8–1	26. ♭3–♭6–2–5
7. 1–♭3–5–♭7	17. 1–5–♭6–4	27. 4–2–♭3–♭7
8. 1–5–4–♭3	18. 1–8–♭7–♭6	28. 5–♭7–8–1
9. 1–♭6–♭7–8	19. 1–4–♭6–8	29. ♭6–4–1–♭3
10. 1–♭7–5–1	20. 1–♭3–2–♭6	30. ♭7–8–♭3–1

Intervals

An *interval* is the distance between two notes. As we've seen, scales are built using intervals of whole and half steps. However, when intervals get larger—as they do when we start singing melodies or chords—we more commonly describe them in terms of *size* (2nd, 3rd, 4th, 5th, 6th, 7th, or 8th) and *quality* (major, minor, perfect, diminished, or augmented).

Size = Number of scale tones or letter names. (Count 'em.)

C to D = 2nd	C to A = 6th
C to E = 3rd	C to B = 7th
C to F = 4th	C to C = 8th (octave)
C to G = 5th	

Quality = sound, or number of whole and half steps

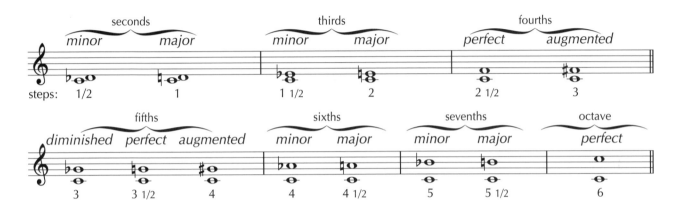

Diatonic Intervals (Ascending & Descending)

The following major key exercise makes use of all the intervals just described (except for major and minor seconds). Sing it with numbers. These intervals are diatonic; that is, they belong to a single key. Therefore, you can focus on either the scale degrees or on the intervals between them.

9 THIRDS

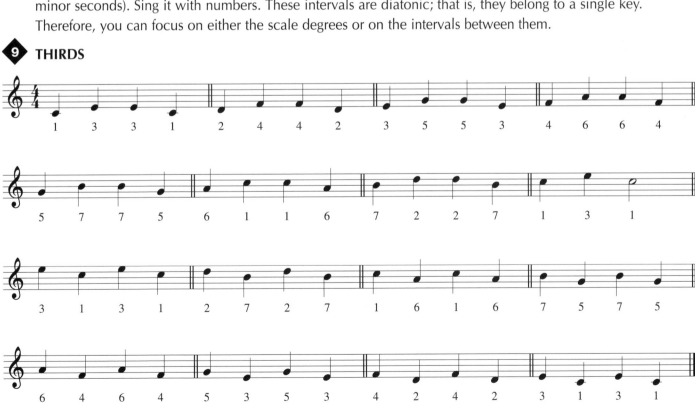

SEVENTHS

1 7 2 1 3 2 4 3 5 4 6 5 7 6 1 7

6 7 5 6 4 5 3 4 2 3 1 2 7 1 7 1

Chromatic Intervals (Ascending)

Now let's try chromatic intervals. These are intervals without a tonal center. Listen to each interval, then sing it back. Use a neutral syllable like "la" or "doo." Concentrate on feeling the interval.

SECONDS

major

minor

THIRDS

major

minor

FOURTHS

perfect

augmented (tritone)

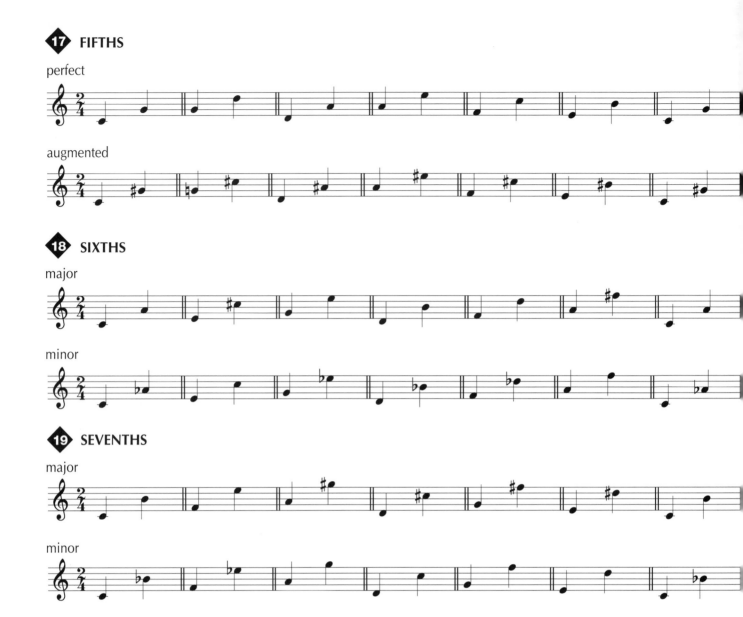

17 ► FIFTHS

perfect

augmented

18 ► SIXTHS

major

minor

19 ► SEVENTHS

major

minor

Song Association

One way to relate to different intervals is to associate them with the first two notes of a song. For instance, an example of an ascending minor 3rd would be "Georgia On My Mind," the Ray Charles classic. An example of a minor 3rd going down would be "Hey Jude" by the Beatles. Check out your own favorite songs, and make your own list of intervals, both ascending and descending. Here's a list to get you started:

	ascending	*descending*
Minor 2nd	Theme from "Jaws"	Stella by Starlight
Major 2nd	Happy Birthday	Three Blind Mice
Minor 3rd	Georgia on My Mind	Hey Jude
Major 3rd	Kum Ba Yah	Summertime
Perfect 4th	Here Comes the Bride	Old McDonald
Aug 4th/Dim 5th	Theme from "The Simpsons"	Guitar riff from YYZ (Rush)
Perfect 5th	Twinkle Twinkle Little Star	Theme from "The Flinstones"
Minor 6th	The Entertainer	Love Story
Major 6th	My Bonnie	Nobody Knows the Trouble I've Seen
Minor 7th	Somewhere (Leonard Bernstein)	Guitar riff from Purple Haze
Major 7th	Theme from "Superman"	I Love You (Cole Porter)
Perfect Octave	Somewhere Over the Rainbow	Willow Weep for Me

This, along with ear training exercises, will help you to "hear" these intervals and to create your own harmony parts.

Inverting Intervals

To invert an interval, take the upper note and move it an octave below (or take the lower note and move it an octave above).

Some interesting things happen when you invert intervals:

1. *Size:* Seconds become sevenths, thirds become sixths, fourths become fifths, fifths become fourths, sixths become thirds, sevenths become seconds. Check it out: Any interval and its inversion add up to the number "9."

2. *Quality:* Major becomes minor, and minor becomes major. Perfect remains perfect, and a tritone remains a tritone. (A tritone is a raised 4th or a lowered 5th.)

To really know this information, you should sing inverted intervals as part of your daily routine. You can practice them in your car, in the shower, or wherever. (Practice them once in a while with a piano, guitar, or the CD—to make sure you're singing and hearing them correctly.) This is all a part of what we call "ear training"—training yourself to "sing what you hear."

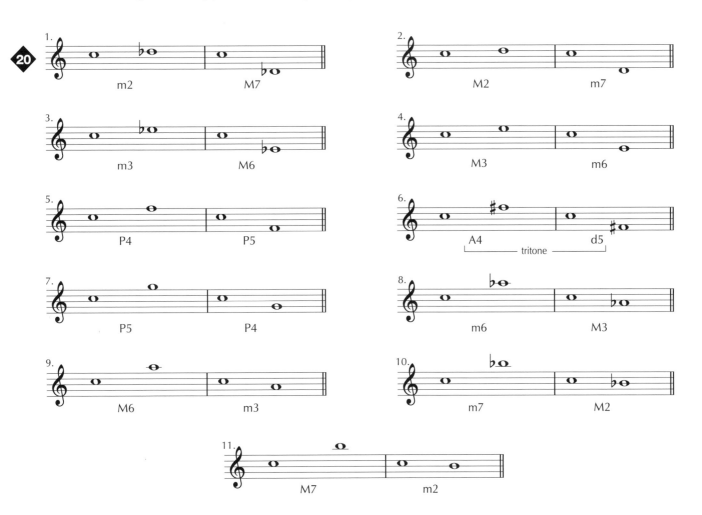

Chords

Intervals are the building blocks of chords, and chords are the building blocks of harmony. A *chord* consists of three or more notes, usually stacked in thirds:

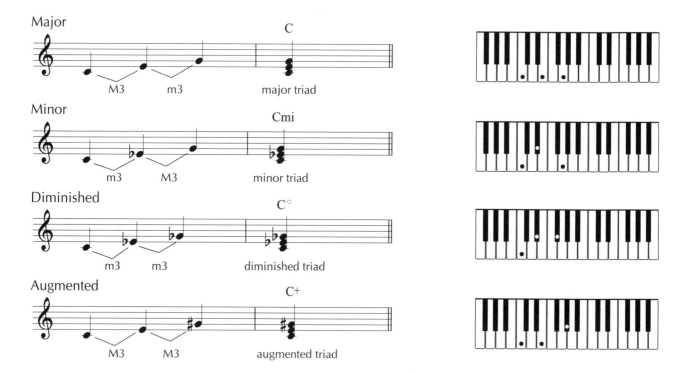

Three-note chords like the ones above are called *triads.* They consist of a *root, 3rd,* and *5th.* If we add another note, a third above, it would be a 7th—giving us a *seventh chord.*

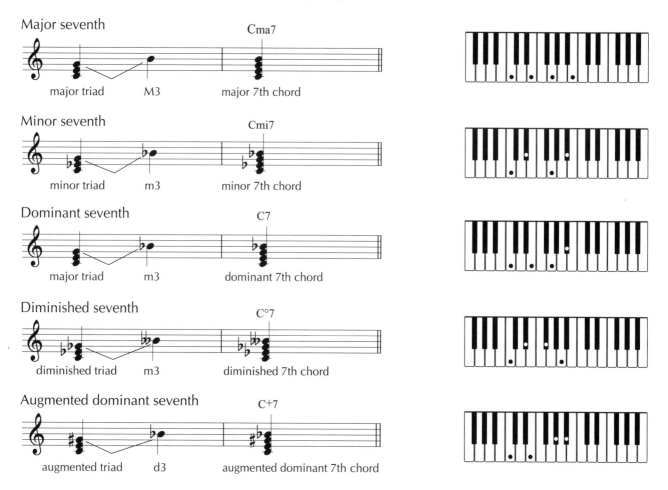

Seventh Chords & Their Inversions

Just as you can invert intervals, you can invert chords, rearranging the notes in relation to one another while still keeping the same basic harmony. In this exercise, we'll sing the chords Cma7, Cmi7, C7, C°7, and C+7, and their inversions. Use a piano or the CD to make sure you're truly singing these chords in tune. This isn't something you can accomplish overnight, so be patient with yourself. Sing the numbers, and don't forget to try these in other keys.

By the way, when more notes are added to a seventh chord, they're generally called *extensions*—these include the 9th, 11th, and 13th, and their sharped or flatted alterations. While these notes add color to the chord, they don't change its fundamental quality. The same notes can be added to or substituted for other notes within a triad, in which case they might be referred to as the 2nd, 4th, and 6th, respectively.

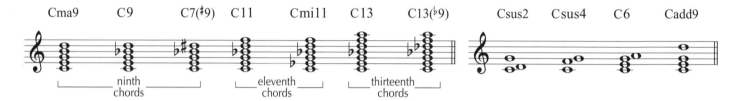

Building Harmonies

Most pop music is what is called "homophonic music," in that there is a strong main melody and the rest of the parts serve as accompaniment. Now that you're fully immersed in learning to sing intervals and chords, your next question might be, "How do I harmonize a melody?"

The answer to that question is simple and not so simple. Music harmony and theory are full of "rules" for building harmony parts and lines. Thankfully, many of these rules have changed along the way as music has evolved, and so those rules are constantly being broken and rewritten. However, there are some teachings that can give you a good start on building good, basic harmony parts.

Major and Minor Key Harmony

Harmonizing each note in a C major scale—first in triads, then in seventh chords—gives us the following chord sequences:

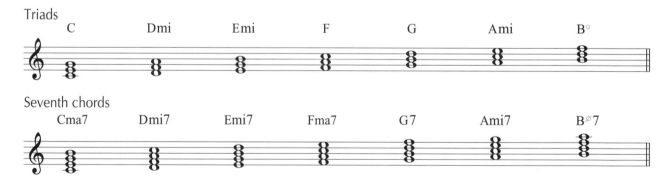

These are the chords diatonic to the key of C major—they're built entirely using notes of the C major scale. Just as the whole-and-half-step formula is the same for any major scale, this chord formula is also the same for any major key, regardless of the tonic. It's often expressed in Roman numerals:

I–IImi–IIImi–IV–V–VImi–VII°

Rearranging these chords to start on the 6th scale degree gives us the chords for the relative minor (in this case, A minor). Realize, this is the same sequence of chord qualities, just starting from a different tonic:

Imi–II°–♭III–IVmi–Vmi–♭VI–♭VII

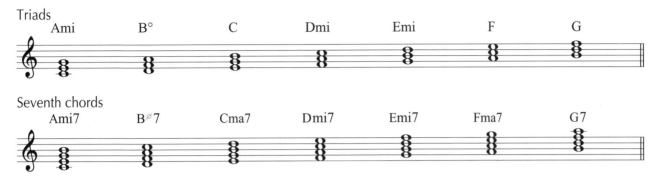

Why know this? Well, these are the chord qualities that you'll most likely be drawing from when singing vocal harmony. They're diatonic; that is, they're within a single key and sound consonant and pleasant. Not all of them, of course, will be used in every song—usually a song or progression will consist of just a few chords, and those are the harmonies you'll be working with. (Please keep in mind, melodies may move very quickly, but chords tend to move slowly—every half measure, every measure, or slower. Not every note of a melody requires its own harmony.)

The bottom line: If you know the key of a song or progression, keep your harmonies within that key and you'll be harmonizing diatonically—and sounding good.

Blues

The blues is one popular exception to diatonic harmony. Most commonly based on a strong I-IV-V progression, the blues favors the sound of the dominant seventh for each of these chords (e.g., C7-F7-G7 in the key of C), rather than their naturally occuring diatonic qualities (e.g., Cma7-Fma7-G7):

Sometimes, determining the key of a song is difficult; perhaps the song contains chords outside the key, modulates frequently, is modal, or operates on a unique set of harmonic rules (like the blues). Even in these cases, there are some good guidelines for you to follow…

Think Chords

The most basic rule of harmony is: *match the chord over which you're singing.* You want to follow the chord progression laid out by the instrumentation. Most of the time, you're going to be singing the 1st, 3rd, or 5th degree of a chord, whether it's major or minor, but remember that not all chords are built that simply. You could be singing over a diminished or augmented chord, or a 7th or 9th chord, so you have to find notes that fit these chords well and build a pleasant sound—if a pleasant sound is what you're after. Experiment with the notes in the chord to find something that's harmonically correct and sounds good.

It used to be that harmonies in pop songs sounded very smooth and didn't use enharmonic tones, but today, just about anything goes.

Pop vs. Choir

Building vocals for pop music is a bit different than building for a choir or *a cappella* group. In *a cappella* or choir, the music is built with the voices serving as all instruments, so those parts need to be arranged to build the chord structure of the song and create a total musical picture. In building harmonies for backing vocals or pop group singing, the instrumentation is usually already in place, so the chord structure is built in.

Think Intervals

Chords are the surest way to harmonize a tune, but constantly referring to them can be cumbersome at times. What if you have a melody with no harmony indicated? In such cases, it can helpful to just focus on singing intervals against the melody. The most common intervals for harmony singing are the 3rd and its inversion the 6th. (It's no coincidence that these are the most common intervals in chord building!)

After that, the 5th and its inversion the 4th would be likely candidates...

And the 7th and its inversion the 2nd.

Of course, you'll likely mix these intervals when creating your own harmonies; this will give your lines some flavor and identity of their own, separating them from the main melody. Generally speaking, consecutive (or "parallel") thirds and sixths are acceptable from time to time, but consecutive 5ths or 4ths are a "no-no." However, even that rule is breakable: There's a recently released song by a girl group in which the girls sing parallel 5ths over a funky hip-hop beat, and it sounds great.

Think Melody

Whether thinking of keys, chords, or intervals, you should also consider the melodic identity of your harmony part(s). How well does each part hold up on its own? Is that important to you? The main melody has an identity—that's what makes it memorable. How your parts interact with the main melody or with each other is a factor that determines their effectiveness.

Parallel motion. This is when all of the parts move in the same direction, either up or down, in the same inversion configuration. This is good for very short backing parts, parts that repeat a word or short phrase of the lead line, or just chime in from time to time. For example, if the chords to a song are C-D-F, then you want to use the 1st, 3rd, and 5th of those chords to build your harmony on.

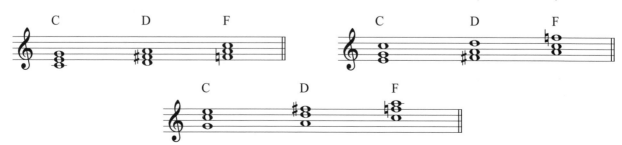

This sounds nice and simple at first, but remember that chords change, and if you use that combination throughout the song, your backing vocals will sound more like a bunch of chanting monks than a hit record. (Well, okay, chanting monks *did* have a hit record, but that is not the sound most people are going for. You typically need to build the lines in different ways and with different rhythms to make them more interesting.)

Contrary motion. This is where all of the parts move in different directions, especially the center part(s). So while the line of the top voice may go down, the center voice would come up and almost meet—and in some cases even cross—the upper part (although crossing parts has traditionally been taboo).

The bottom line motion could depend on the bass line of the instrumentation or how many parts you have in the center.

Oblique motion is when some parts stay stationary, singing one note that is common to all the chords, while the other parts move. For example, in the following progression, the top and middle voices move while the bottom voice remains on the note G throughout.

A common use of oblique motion is when the bass holds one note while the other voices move, creating slash chords.

Both contrary and oblique motion are ideal for backing vocals where the lead vocal is singing something different from the backing vocals, where the backing vocals are holding the meat of the chorus while the lead vocal improvises, and, of course, in vocal groups.

Remember that you don't have to stick with just one way of singing harmonies in a song. One part may use a simple parallel motion and another part continuous harmony lines using oblique or contrary motion. Even the rules like "no parallel 4ths or 5ths" are up for interpretation, so you can use this as a starting point; the rest is up to you.

2 TIPS & TECHNIQUES
How to Sing Like a Pro

Learning to read notes, recognize intervals, and sing scales and chords will be a tremendous help to you in singing backing vocals; having these skills will allow you to become a true professional in the field and will separate you from many of the other singers out there trying to do the same. But they are only part of learning to sing backing vocals. There are many other techniques and tricks that can help you stand out and blend in, making you a great backing vocalist.

For all singers, there are two main arenas: the studio and the stage. Techniques for singing on stage and singing in the studio can vary greatly. What is passable on stage often will not fly in the studio because of the sensitivity of the microphones. Popping consonants, ragged breathing, or ever-so-slightly-off entrances and exits will show up with much more clarity. On the other hand, lack of excitement, not being "into" what you're doing, or not being part of the musical unit will show up much more on stage. In live performance, you cannot give another singer a sour look, and you cannot stop. There are no "do-overs." But regardless of whether you are on stage or in the studio, you must do your best to make the unit, either live band or recording, sound as good as possible.

Cohesiveness of the Backing Vocal

As a backing vocalist, it's unlikely that you'll be working alone. Sure, occasionally on a recording, a producer might use one singer to do all of the backing parts, but in live performance that's not possible, so you must always remember that you are part of a unit and that unit should function like a well-oiled machine.

There are many things you can do to assure that your part of the unit is working properly. The biggest common denominator, live or in the studio, the most important skill, is *the ability to listen*. You might be a great singer, but if you cannot listen and blend with the other backing vocalists, you may as well go home. We can't stress this enough.

There's a woman we know who has a tremendous voice, a beautiful sound, but she has a very hard time singing with others. She's always in tune and always has her part, and she sounds great on backing vocals in the studio, if the parts are put down one at a time. But in live performance, she sticks out like a sore thumb—because she doesn't listen to the others she is singing with; she simply sings her part as loud as she can. This is a nightmare for the engineers, the other singers, and the overall sound of the live performance.

What is it you're supposed to be listening for? Many things, but what follows are a few items that we feel are particularly important, which will get you through rehearsals, sessions, and performances—these are techniques, tricks, and common sense to help you get your chops together and get you through the rough spots.

Blend

What is blend? Blend is the balance of sound within the group; which of your singers is the strongest, which is the weakest. Remember, the group is only as strong as your weakest singer, because the group dynamic is dependent on the possibility of the singers' vocals having equal weight. Can you hear everyone? Does any part stick out more than the other? Is that the intended effect? It's not necessary that everyone have the same volume—a bass voice may need to be a bit more intense than the rest of the group in order for the group to sound balanced.

Balancing voices in a vocal arrangement can be as harrowing as balancing on a high wire. The type of voices that carry sound farthest must be mindful of their volume. Tenors and sopranos can easily "take over" the sound, leaving the altos and basses in the sonic dustbin. The same holds true of anyone with a strong voice.

Learn to listen to your own voice twice. First, listen for the tonal quality (pitch, dynamic quality). Then, listen to make sure it's not overwhelming the others in the group. Practicing dynamic changes and control will help with this. Can you raise or lower the volume without completely changing your tone quality? Perhaps a change in quality would enhance the sound of the group. Experimenting in rehearsal is the only way to find out about the group dynamic.

Hearing Other Vocalists...On Stage

First of all, if you cannot hear the other singers on stage—unless you have a horrible monitor, which can be the case—you're singing too loudly. You should be able to hear the parts that the other backing vocalists are singing in addition to your own part. When singing on stage, if you can't hear the other singers, back off a little bit, soften up if you can. When you're singing live, depending on the quality of the equipment, the size of the venue, and the acoustics of the room, you may have to make some radical adjustments to your sound.

Make sure you've located the monitors, and learn to train yourself on them. In most cases, the monitors will be on the floor in front of you, but there are times when they'll be mounted above your head, so the first thing you should do is make sure you know where they are. If you're holding the microphone in your hand, it is very important that you do not point the microphone into the monitor. This usually causes feedback and annoys the engineer to the point of exhaustion.

It's not uncommon for singers to forget themselves and let that microphone drop to their side and point directly into the monitor, so you must remain aware of what you're doing if you are holding the microphone in your hand. A good rule of thumb is to hold the microphone at chest-level when you're not singing into it. The squeal of feedback is one of the most unpleasant sounds I can think of, and it can do some damage to your hearing in the long run. Loud feedback can also temporarily throw your hearing off and cause you to sing out of tune, so please be aware of yourself and the microphone.

Depending on the type of microphone you're using, you can use your body position to adjust the sound. If you're using a *dynamic microphone,* you can be as much as 6 inches from the microphone and still be heard if you're singing loudly. But remember that dynamic microphones pick up the sound of the instruments around you, so if you aren't singing "a cappella," this may not be the best solution. *Condenser microphones* are usually better for a situation where there is a band behind you, but if your mouth is more than 1 inch away from the ball of the microphone, the sound may cut in and out. We've heard singers who are used to working with the older type of microphones try to "work" the condenser microphone in the same way. The result can border on the comic. Words and music get lost, and the overall performance suffers. It's important that you understand a little bit of microphone technology so you know what type of microphone you're using and what it will and won't do. If you are using a condenser microphone, try to sing more dynamically and keep your microphone position somewhat stable.

When sharing a microphone in live singing, you must be very close to your singing partner. (Don't be afraid, and try to make sure your breath is fresh!) Depending on the quality and type of microphone, most stage microphones pick up sound best from the front of the microphone ball, so singing into the sides is not very effective. You need to have both mouths as close to the center of the microphone as possible. Adjust your voice or body for blend depending on the type of microphone. Dynamic microphones work best in this situation, as they will pick up more sound at greater distances, but there may be some instrument bleeding into the mics. If you have superior equipment and are using *overhead microphones,* simply position yourselves so the microphone hangs between you.

Hearing Other Vocalists... In the Studio

If you're working in the studio, and each vocalist has their own microphone, you can ask the engineer to turn other vocals up in the headphone mix, or turn the music down. Another thing you can do is take one side of the headphones off and see if it helps you hear the other vocalists a little better. If you do take one side of the headphones off, remember to turn it so it's flush against your head; otherwise, the sounds coming through the headphone will bleed into the microphone.

If you're all singing on one microphone in the studio, proper *positioning* is very important. In live performance, you'll most likely have your own microphone (unless you're singing with a choir), so the positioning of the singers is not so significant, but in recording it's vital. If you have a good engineer or producer, they will position you after hearing the blend of voices to better balance the sound, but sometimes you will have to do the positioning yourself.

A good guide to go by is this: Alto, baritone, and bass voices tend to get lost faster than soprano and tenor voices, because higher tones cut through the music easier than lower tones. If your sopranos have particularly large voices, you'll want to place them farther back in the group or more to the sides and your warmer quieter voices in the middle, so that the blend is more even. Of course, voices vary, so you'll want to experiment and find the positions that give your group the most balanced sound. Unless you're doing the recording yourself, leave the final decisions on who should adjust what volumes and positions up to the producer or engineer. They are in the control booth and know just how much of whom they want to hear, so don't try to second guess them; just try as hard as you can to give them what they want.

Once you have your positions set, either by the engineer or by the group, and everyone is satisfied with the sound, make sure you do not move, unless you're asked to. Even if you take a break, it is important to remember where you're standing, so that you'll get the same blend when you continue. You may ask the engineer to place a small piece of tape on the floor for you to mark your spot. I know someone who does a lot of group work, and she carries a small pad of Post-It notes in her bag. When the positioning is done, she gives each person a Post-It with their initials on it and has them place it at their toes so that everyone can remember their position.

Next, you should be listening for *timing.* Are you coming in on exactly the right beat? Are you and the other vocalists cutting off at the same point, or are some of the cut-offs ragged or out of time? Even if you've rehearsed well, this is sometimes overlooked and can make a backing vocal sound sloppy. It's occasionally a good idea to put one of the vocalists in charge of guiding entrances and cut-offs. The vocalist in charge can use their hands to help guide the others so the entrances are on time and the cut-offs are smooth. After using this technique a few times, the entrances and exits should go smoothly, and the group will no longer need a guide.

Another thing you want to listen for is *accents.* Are any of the words being "punched"? Punching a word is adding a little volume and velocity so the word stands out. Which words are smooth and soft? What part of the verse has a greater volume level, a lift? Are the notes in any particular passage even, or swelled? Are you singing "full voice" or soft and airy? Deciding on these actions and remembering what you decided is one of the things that give the backing vocal its life.

Staying On Your Part

Remember that, in singing harmonies or backing vocals, you are part of the instrumentation, part of the music as a whole, and your role is the same as that of a guitarist, bassist, or keyboardist. Consider your part your own melody. Sing it as if it is *the* melody. While you are trying to blend with the other vocalists, you have to be strong and certain of your notes and where they go, so if you give your part the same weight or importance as the melody, it'll be easier for you to remember it and keep it.

One of the common difficulties in singing group harmonies is keeping your own part. It's almost certain that an inexperienced singer will "slip" into the part of the person standing next to them, or whichever part is the most prominent, often without even realizing they've done so. Sonically, the highest part is the easiest to hear, the higher tones cutting through the others, and singers trying to hold a middle or bottom part other than the melody will often slip into the higher part. Spending some time singing with a choir can strengthen your ability so stay on your part, so will ear training and sightsinging exercises. The more you practice, the better you'll be.

In the studio, getting a better headphone mix will usually help this situation. Ask the engineer to put a little more of you in your headphones. If you're singing in a group situation in the studio, removing one side of your headphones will not only help you hear yourself, it can help you hear how well you're blending, too. In a live singing situation, if you cannot hear yourself well or are standing next to someone with a strong voice or standout part, we hate to say it, but plug up an ear. While this is not the most professional-looking move, we'd rather see a plugged ear than hear a bad note.

Finding your pitches in the instrumentation can help you remain in your part; find an instrument that's playing your tones, such as the bass if you're singing the bass part. The instrument may not be playing the same line you're singing, but it may play an "anchor note" that you can use as a reference point for your part. It's important to latch onto an instrument that has a repeating part, so that the reference occurs frequently. You may not need to use this trick forever, but it can be a great help if you're new to singing harmonies.

Pronunciation

Pronunciation is also a key factor in having a smooth, professional sound in your backing vocals. There are many words that have their accents on different syllables and even have different speech melodies depending on what country you're from, or even which part of the U.S. you live in. How you pronounce a word also can give it the effect of being a more casual vocal, a straight pop sound, or an R&B sound. Take the word "baby" for example: Some pronounce it "bay-bee," while others might prefer "bay-bay" or "bay-buh." It's really up to the leader, or producer, which sound is most appropriate, but once the decision is made, it's important for all of the singers to render the same pronunciation.

Another part of the pronunciation problem is endings. Often, if a word ends in "s" or "t" or some other strong consonant sound, the effect of too many people ending in a slightly different place can make the vocal sound sloppy or unprofessional. One common solution, if you're singing in a group, is to have everyone in the group sing the word minus the ending consonant, except one or two people. For example, if your phrase ends in the word "grows," only one person in a group of four would form the "s" at the end of the word. This works well in the studio when you have many people singing one part on each track.

One exception in pronunciation is when you're going for a "choir" sound. It's often the differences in these things that give a choir a more rich and fat sound, especially a gospel choir sound. If you know the producer is trying for a choir sound, ask her or him what their preferences are.

Holding long vowels can also cause problems if the singers do not have the same pronunciation. Long notes have a tendency to mutate a little, and if the vowels start off a little different, they can end up very different. Again, check the pronunciation with all members of the group or the producer, make a decision about it, and stick to it.

Vibrato

Vibrato is one of the things that gives a voice its personality and color. It can be a wonderful, useful part of your voice, or it can be a nightmare. Some people cannot find their vibrato. There are different types of vibrato, and no two singers have exactly the same vibrato. One type of vibrato is a manufactured trill most often used by classically trained singers that involves manipulating the diaphragm to form the sound variation. The other is a natural wobble that can occur when the voice is making a tone and the throat is relaxed and the air is balanced.

We cannot tell you what's best for you personally, but whatever type of vibrato you have, it is important to be aware of it and have control over it for backing vocals in the studio. At times, a nice, warm vibrato is the preferred sound, but other times too many different rates of vibrato speed can cause a wobbling effect and make the vocals sound off pitch. It's often desirable that the vibratos of the singers in the session match as closely as possible. But every voice is different, so how can they? Some singers can control the *rate of vibrato* and use that control to match the vibrato of other singers. This is a very valuable skill to have if you plan on being a professional backing vocalist.

It is possible to learn to control your vibrato. This can be difficult at first, but with practice you can master including and removing your vibrato at will, and controlling the speed of the vibrato. You can work on this any number of ways; here's one exercise:

- Sound a note in a comfortable pitch for you. Keep the tone as clear and open as you can.

- Now sing the tone again, this time keeping the tone straight, with no vibrato. Hold the note for as long as you can without the sound deteriorating.

- Sound the note once more. Allow the vibrato to form. Now, while keeping the flow of air constant, smoothly remove the vibrato, making a straight clear note.

- Breathe. Now begin with a clear vibrato-less note. Make sure the note is strong and the airflow is consistent. Now add a slow vibrato, gradually increasing the rate of speed.

- Repeat this exercise for 10-15 minutes daily.

There are other techniques to help you find, diminish, or control your vibrato, but they require the supervision of a vocal instructor to assure that you're doing them properly. If you find this exercise too difficult, consult your vocal instructor. He or she may be able to help you successfully execute the exercise, or may have other techniques that can assist you in accomplishing this goal.

The Overall Vibe

The "vibe" of a tune is not just about the notes; it's about the *feeling* of the material as well. For example, if you're singing a song that's upbeat and joyous, nothing kills it faster than a lifeless, lackluster backing vocal. It's just as important for the backing vocalists to find the happiness, sadness, anger or the passion in a song as it is for the lead vocalist. Remember that you're helping to carry the musical vibe, and often you're weaving a carpet for the lead vocalist to ride on, to soar upon. You're providing a solid base over which the lead vocalist can improvise, while insuring that the vocal integrity of the song remains intact. You may be keeping the main melody going, adding a second important message to the song, or filling up the instrumentation. So just as the musicians playing the song have to find the "groove," so must the backing vocalist. If the song has a laid-back feel, you must try to find that groove, or if you're singing a rock tune that is well on top of the beat, your vocals must also be on top of the beat. Occasionally a novice vocalist may get lost, forget their part, or stray onto the part of another singer, but in live performance, if the overall vibe and energy is kept, the audience will probably never notice.

Vocal Effects

Often, the inexperienced vocalist will assume that as long as they are heard, what they are doing is okay. In fact, there are many types of vocal effects you can use, or that a producer may ask you to employ. Especially in backing vocals and group singing, it's not always appropriate for you to sing at a normal volume or with a standard amount of intensity. It may be necessary to modify the volume and intensity of your singing to fit the mood, music level, and section of the piece you are performing. Here are some explanations of the most commonly used vocal effects and dynamics.

Soft Vocal

A soft vocal is one that is normal in intensity and low in volume. It's not airy and whispery, but resembles a low speaking voice. This gives the vocals a solid quality without overpowering the lead vocal. Practice talking in a soft speaking voice just above a whisper, engaging some of the vocal cord.

How to practice the soft vocal: Pick a phrase or song lyric and simply speak it low, but at the same pitch that you would sing it. Now sing the phrase with the same intensity you just spoke—soft but not overly airy. The desired result is a sound that is light and clear, but in no way loud.

Whisper or Airy Vocal

The whisper vocal, or airy vocal, employs less intensity of cord than the soft vocal and an overabundance of air as well. This production can add an ethereal quality to a song, making it more heavenly, or give it a sensual quality, making it more intimate. It is sung just like a spoken whisper, but with just enough vocal cord intensity to hold the tone. It's an important quality to practice, often used in the early verses or choruses of a song, in love songs, or songs with an ethereal quality. Practicing this technique is highly recommended, because the breathy quality can sometimes result in a loss of pitch control, since almost none of the vocal cord is engaged.

How to practice the airy vocal: Pick a phrase or song lyric and simply speak it low but at the same pitch that you would sing it. Now add a considerable amount of air. Do not add so much air that the tone of the voice disappears, because you must also hold this air while singing specific pitches. If you no longer have tone in your speaking voice, adjust the airflow down until tone returns. Now sing the phrase with the same intensity you just spoke it. The desired result is a sound that is light and breezy, sexy, or sweet, depending on the inflections. The airy vocal must be produced by keeping only the slightest edge of cord and a tremendous amount of airflow. Limit practice of this technique to a few minutes a day, as it can be drying to the throat.

Full Voice

Singing full voice is singing in your most natural voice, the one that is closest to your basic speaking voice. The range of the full voice depends on the natural abilities and vocal training of the individual. Good production of full voice is that which is not strained or pushed, but has an open and resonant sound. It is not usually desirable to have a pushed or forced sound in group singing, so it's important in group singing to know what your range is in full and head voice productions, so that you can be assigned a part that's comfortable for you to sing.

Finding the range for your natural full voice is fairly simple:

Find the lowest note you can comfortably sing, still maintaining reasonable volume and fullness. (Once the voice becomes barely audible or too shaky, do not consider these notes as part of your full voice range. Although you may hit them in some way, they will probably not be usable in singing your parts, especially in the recording studio, where the microphones are so sensitive that they pick up every breath and will show the weakness of the voice.) From that lowest usable tone, sing up either in diatonic scale form or chromatically until you reach a point where you cannot comfortably produce a pleasant tone with reasonable volume. If the tone is produced only with a considerable amount of strain and the volume is uncontrollable, you have surpassed the top of your full voice range.

While this range is expandable with proper training, you must learn to use what you have at the moment and consider using only what will sound good.

The Edgy Vocal

The edgy vocal is most often reserved for the lead vocal of a song; however, in R&B, rock, or gospel singing groups such as the Temptations, Four Tops, or modern groups like En Vogue or Brownstone, this type of vocal can add character and grit to what might otherwise be a bland production. While it would obviously be better if the vocalist had a naturally gritty or raspy voice, there are many ways to produce a gritty sound. There are several ways to produce this sound in a healthy and proper manner; however, done wrong, these effects can be damaging, so to give you a method of practice here could be irresponsible. It would be advisable to find an instructor who can teach you to produce the effect in your soft palate at the back of the tongue, rather than in the center or base of the throat, thereby diminishing or eliminating the possibility of cord damage.

 We recommend that anyone who plans on being a professional singer consult a vocal instructor at least once in their lifetime. A qualified instructor will be able to tell you if you're using your voice in a healthy way, or if you're doing anything that can cause vocal damage. A good teacher can also help you to find out things about your voice you never knew, find things you didn't know your voice would do, point out ways to improve your sound, give you a warm-up and practice routine, and give you tools to help keep your voice healthy and strong for decades. There are healthier ways of making even the most raunchy rock 'n' roll sounds, and a qualified instructor can help you accomplish these things.

Falsetto

Falsetto tones are more commonly employed by the male voice when producing high pitches. While there are many who do not consider the female voice capable of producing true falsetto—only head voice—for the sake of explaining the effect, we will assume that it can. The falsetto effect is high tones produced with neither too much air nor too much cord involvement, resulting in a high, thin sound that can most often be characterized as pure. It can be produced loudly or softly, thin (falsetto degola) or fat (falsetto detesta).

How do you find your falsetto? Well it's the voice that you use when imitating a mouse or some other small creature. Listen to the voice of Mickey Mouse; that's a person speaking in falsetto. Many singers have made their living using this voice. Singers like Al Green, The Gibb brothers of the BeeGees, Roland Gift of Fine Young Cannibals, Michael Jackson, and Prince use their falsetto on a regular basis. Also singers such as Whitney Houston, Mariah Carey, and Vonda Shepard use this voice to get that soft high sound.

Practice and Rehearsal

Once you have a solid foundation in singing harmonies and you want to join a group, form a group, or sing backing vocals for another artist, there are many methods of rehearsing, with many levels of implementation:

- First and foremost, be as prepared as possible. If you're putting together a performance and have control over when you get the charts and/or tapes of the song(s) you're going to perform, you can make sure everyone in the group has the information well ahead of the first rehearsal. Knowing who sings best in what range is essential; then the parts can be pre-assigned, and all of the singers will get an opportunity to look over and practice the material prior to the first rehearsal.

- If you only have charts, learn your part as if it were the melody, and also learn the melody of the tune so you have a reference point for your part. If you also have the recorded music, practice your melodies and timing to the track; you may even record yourself singing the parts to the track to ensure they're well in tune and rhythm. Practice the parts with different dynamic qualities, because you never know what will sound best until you are blending with the other voices.

- As a group, try to rehearse in a place that allows you to hear each other well—so that you limit mistakes and vocal strain—and has enough space that you can see each other as well. Some of the best places to practice are unusual, like a large bathroom or the top of a stairwell. These places have natural echo effects and can make practicing more enjoyable. Make sure your practice space has plenty or air, because so many people singing in one small enclosed space is not healthy. The air can become bad very quickly, and the members of your group will begin to run out of energy. If you have to practice in a small, poorly ventilated space, you must take frequent breaks to "air out" the room.

- Once the vocal parts are together and sounding sweet, if you know the formation of the group on stage or in the studio—meaning how and where you will be standing—practice that way. Standing in a different place than usual, or losing eye contact with the other vocalists, can change your aural perspective and make it more difficult to maintain the sound you've worked so hard for.

This may seem like too many precautions and overkill, but if you plan on making a career out of singing harmony vocals, you must make sure that you are at all time prepared and professional.

At the end of all of the exercises and practicing opportunities, if you've done your homework, you should have a firm grasp on singing harmony vocals and on what to do and not to do in professional situations. Remember that, in the end, the person who gets hired is the one who sings well, clear, is always prepared, and does not waste valuable time, whether it is their own or someone else's. Friendliness, patience, a good attitude, and professionalism are essential. There are many people who make a great living singing in the background, touring, and making a lot of money without the hassles of being the "star." Some people who sing commercials have made in the neighborhood of a million dollars a year, give or take a few thousand. Then, of course there are all the groups: Manhattan Transfer, Sweet Honey and the Rock, Boyz II Men, Take 6, Boyzone, Backstreet Boys, SWV, Eternal, En Vogue. The list is endless, and so are your possibilities if you're serious about what you do and you work hard.

3 SONGBITES
For Practicing 3-Part Harmony

Practicing scales, intervals, and chords will help you learn to find parts, sing against other notes, and improve your musical knowledge and skills, but the real trick to singing good harmony vocals is singing with other voices. If you have the desire to form or join a vocal group, that's terrific; go for it. Joining a choir can help to familiarize you with singing against other voices and give you a great deal of security and support while you're learning. Unfortunately, not all of us can join a vocal group or choir, and that's where the mini-songs provided on the companion CD come in.

We've recorded eighteen "songbites" in a variety of styles for you to practice with. Some of these are very easy to sing, with easy parts, while others are more difficult and will require more concentration. Each songbite has three-part harmony. The first time through, you'll hear what the harmony should sound like with all three parts present. Then, there are three separate examples, each with a different part taken out so you can practice singing the "missing" harmonies, one at a time. This gives you 56 different harmonizing opportunities! Each part is written out separately, with lyrics, so you can identify the part you're singing and practice your reading skills if you so choose. If a part is too high for you, try singing it an octave lower, or if it's too low, try singing it an octave higher.

These songbites cover a wide range of musical and vocal styles so that you can practice some of the different vocal effects and dynamic variations we talked about earlier. A good way to make sure you're singing correctly is to tape yourself in practice. That way, you can check to hear if what you're singing is correct and sounds good.

Songbite #1

This songbite is in a pop-rock style with a ska influence. Ska music originated in Jamaica in the 1950s as a mixture of a traditional Jamaican music created in the 1920s (called mento) and American R&B. Ska had a limited popularity in the United States and Europe in the 1950s, but its renaissance came in the '70s and '80s when bands like the Specials, Selecter, and Madness resurrected the style. Other musicians, like the Police and Elvis Costello, blended ska with rock music to create a sound that is still fresh today. The second renaissance of ska came from bands like No Doubt.

The vocal in "Doh-Dee-Doh" is a medium-volume full voice but not particularly pretty. In rock vocals, often the sound is purposely "unpretty" to keep the edge of the music. So this type of vocal is very close to a speaking voice.

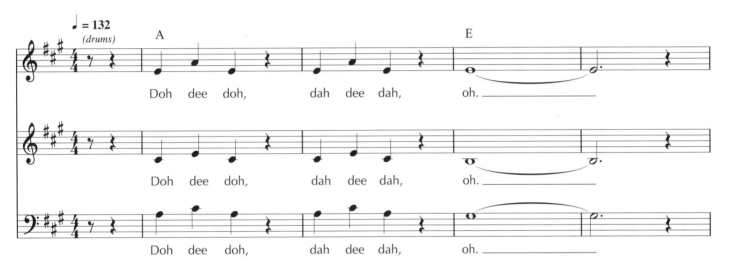

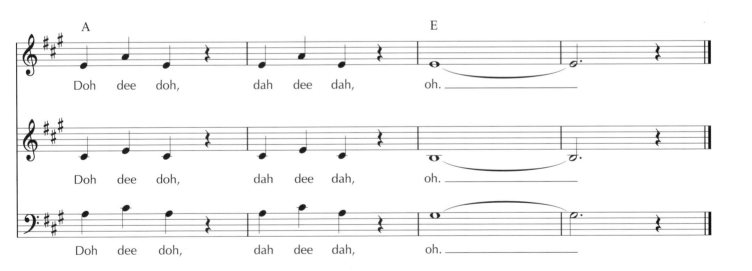

Songbite #2

"Don't Get a Tattoo" is soft modern rock, the type of rock music that grew out of the '80s and early '90s. The vocals are sweet and smooth but also very straight. This kind of smooth vocal is often used as a contrast to the rough or powerful voice of the lead vocalist. Either a soft-volume full voice or a falsetto can be used to create the effect of this smooth vocal. The phrasing is long; no sharp cut-offs or staccato lines.

 # Don't Get a Tattoo

Songbite #3

The '60s rock feel of "London Traffic" is a perfect example of a harmony "gang vocal," where the singers are almost "talk singing." In this type of music, it isn't important that the lead singer has a great voice, just as long as the lyrics are inspiring and/or the playing conveys lots of feeling. (Think of Bob Dylan's brilliant songs, or the music of guitar greats like Jimi Hendrix, Eric Clapton, and Jeff Beck.) It's not important that the backing vocal here be lovely, just on pitch and loud. Attitude is also important. The syllables in "London" are "punched"; in this case, meaning they are staccato with loud accents. The vocal is very dynamic.

London Traffic

Songbite #4

"Tell Your Mama" is '50s blues-based R&B. The flavor is New Orleans, a melding of blues and R&B, rowdy guitars, and rowdy singers. The vocal is sassy; it swings. The second syllable of the word "mama" has an upward slur on the end, giving it a more "greasy" feel. A little more down-and-dirty than traditional doo-wop, it's the kind of gospel-based vocal that artists like Solomon Burke used in their recordings. Lots of vibrato and dynamic, swelling punches make this hybrid of gospel and blues very soulful. This type of vocal eventually became smoother and morphed into groups like the Temptations and the Four Tops.

Tell Your Mama

Songbite #5

Chuck Berry, Little Richard, Carl Perkins, and a host of others who took blues and honky-tonk a lot further are responsible for this '50s rock 'n' roll style. Some was New Orleans style, some Chicago blues mixed with R&B, some had a country influence, but it all had that swing. The backing vocal here represents another type of gang vocal, one that is closer to a group of fans singing in an audience than a group of professionals, but that's the point. The urgency and looseness of the vocal complement the rockin' style and bring the listener into the music. This vocal is high-volume, on-pitch singing with a little bit of yell in it.

Don't Be So Good

Songbite #6

Somewhere in-between '50s rock 'n' roll and smooth, traditional soul doo-wop were groups like the Coasters, who pulled the dreamy sounds of tight harmonies and soaring falsettos into a faster and rompier style. They even brought a lot of humor into the music with songs like "Charlie Brown" and "I've Been Searchin'." The harmonies are still tight, but there's a hint of laughter and mischief in the sound. The vocal is medium-volume full voice or falsetto.

Go Walk the Dog

Songbite #7

The sounds of early '70s funk reflect their R&B and gospel roots in choir-like backing vocals. It's a rich and percussive sound with a little punch—so strong that it's almost a lead vocal. Groups like Graham Central Station, Sly and the Family Stone, and Rufus made this sound fly; the backing vocals hold up the body of the song, which often has more than one lead singer, adding to the feeling of community.

Songbite #8

As with the previous songbite, this is reflective of '70s funk, but more of an old-school piece, a mix between funk and 60's doo-wop groups like the Temptations and the Four Tops. The vocal is strong and percussive instead of smooth, and the beat is definitely funk, but the instrumentation has a sweet-soul, Wilson Pickett, Jackie Wilson feel. This vocal is strong, punchy, and bold.

55 56 57 58 We Can Make It

top out · middle out · bottom out

Songbite #9

The '60s girl group was a natural offshoot of the '50s doo-wop boys. Girl groups began popping up as early as the late '50s, some in the traditional doo-wop style, but more often with one girl singing the lead and the others singing backing vocals. Often the lead vocalists switched off depending on whose voice had the best sound for the song. Girl groups sometimes had a very sweet sound, like the Supremes, the Shirelles, or the Ronettes, but other times they had more of a soul sound like Martha and the Vandellas. This songbite is also based in a gospel sound, like that used by Aretha Franklin. That sound lives today in the girl group renaissance with artists like Destiny's Child, Blaque, En Vogue, and Brownstone.

Ooh, Baby

Songbite #10

Ah, the smooth sounds, the smooth moves, the smooth hair… '50s doo-wop. Beginning with The Ink Spots and The Mills Brothers—the grandfathers of doo-wop—it's a style taken straight from the street corners. From the Drifters to the Dominos, the Platters to the Penguins, the soft blend of majestic harmonies is still making girls swoon today as sung by groups like Boyz II Men, Backstreet Boys, and Boyzone. These harmonies often had a range of voices from the highest, sweetest falsetto to the deepest soul-shaking bass. The vocal may be strong or soft—at times, even a whisper—but is always smooth and tight.

Doo-ee-ooh

Songbite #11

Sometimes vocals are needed to give a feeling of woodwinds or brass when there are none. Such is the example here. Often, you'll sing one word, or something that's not even a word but simply an emulation of another instrument. The music has a smooth modern sound, and the vocals become another instrument. This vocal is sometimes percussive and sometimes smooth. It's syncopated, so pay close attention to the beat on which you come in.

Songbite #12

This kind of modern adult contemporary music is a mixture of sweet '60s soul and jazz, with artists from both categories, like Anita Baker, Al Jarreau, and Oleta Adams, crossing the barriers. A little more sophisticated than straight soul music, the warm light, backing vocals are a perfect complement.

71 72 73 74 You'll Have My Love

top middle bottom
out out out

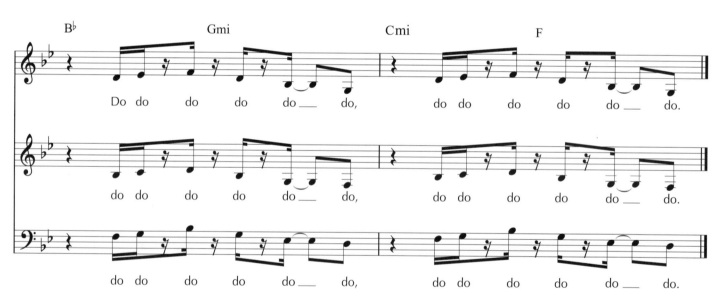

Songbite #13

There is disco, and then there is disco soul. The late '70s gave us a lot of dance music, and this type of music was not just a straight disco beat. It has all the elements of old R&B music wrapped around a faster beat; bass that not only thumps but also grooves. The backing vocals groove as well. Dynamic and punchy, strong soul voices, something between '70s funk groups like Sly and the Family Stone and the girl groups of today. The thing to watch here is the rhythm, the syncopation. If you're too fast, you'll rush it; if you're too slow, it'll drag.

Songbite #14

As with the previous songbite, this is '70s disco soul. This one is a little more straightforward, but not any less funky. The important thing here is to watch the pitch, and sound like you're having fun. Different vibrato rates will not budge the integrity of the vocal here; just remember to punch that beginning "Oh yeah."

Dance, Dance, Dance

Songbite #15

The roots of bluegrass country music are in Scotland and Ireland: fast and furious fiddlin' that everyday folk could dance to. Bill Monroe was one the most popular figures in traditional bluegrass. "Katmandu" is a more modern version of bluegrass, mixed in with the modern country style of such artists as Loretta Lynn and Garth Brooks, who've given the traditional music a new flare. This will give you a chance to practice your twang (but don't overdo it). Listen for the anticipated entrance on the second half of the vocal.

Katmandu

Songbite #16

Country music has taken quite a few turns in the past few decades. Some of it has stayed pretty true to traditional form, but many artists have leaned more towards a blending with pop, folk, or rock 'n' roll. Regardless of what kind of turn it takes, you will always hear the telltale fiddles and slide guitars that are the hallmark of country. Artists like Shania Twain, Kathy Mattea, Mary Chapin Carpenter, Reba McEntire, and Wynonna Judd have given country music a new face, and that's reflected in the more modern sounds of this and the next two songbites.

Business Suit

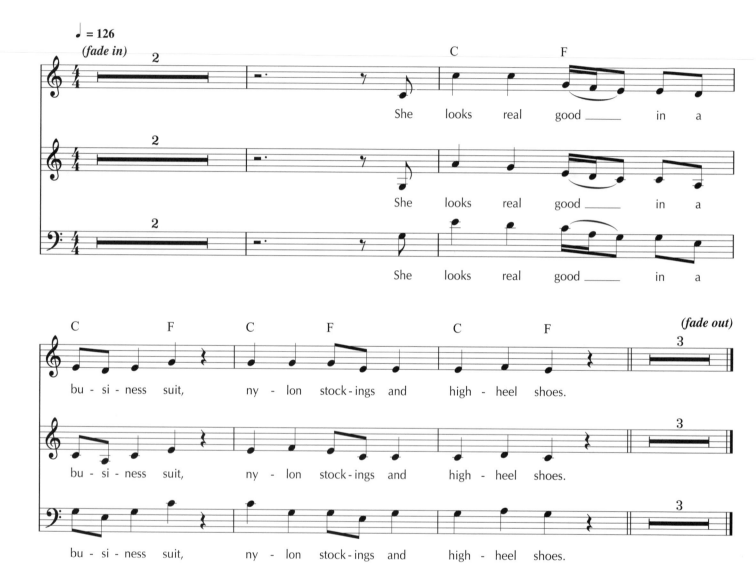

Songbite #17

Repetition is the name of the game when you're singing backing vocals. Making sure those hooks feel like the most important part of the song is all part of the territory. Having the right chorus of voices on the hook can make or break the song.

Songbite #18

There are times when, as a backing vocalist, you will not sing a word—just the sweet ooh's and ah's that help create a seamless segue between the instrumental and the lead vocal. There is no sweeter sound than the blending of voices on pure vowels. The trick here is to keep the voice steady and lively sounding. You have to keep the integrity of the song, the vibe and upbeat feeling, without saying anything at all. So the trick here is attitude and, of course, an open throat.

Country Ahs

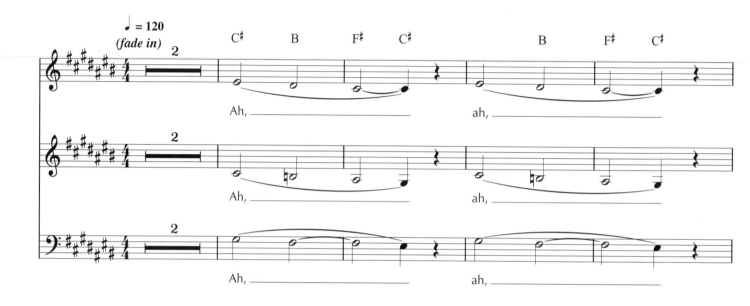

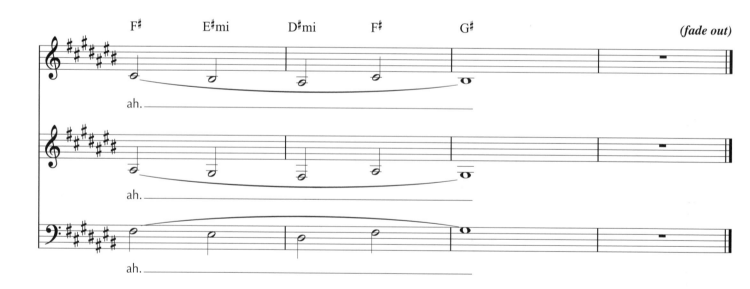

ADVANCED SIGHTSINGING

This section is for advanced singers who want new challenges—or for beginners who want something to aspire to. These are exercises that we, ourselves, have wanted to work on as vocalists. Their purpose is to challenge you melodically, harmonically, and rhythmically. There is no audio for this, so… you're on your own. Find yourself a piano, or get together with a group of other singers, and give 'em a shot. Good luck!

Singing Through Chords

These chord-based melodies are a good way of practicing the different chord qualities we've learned, but in a more musical context—as well as getting used to each chord's position/function within a major key.

Key of C

Key of G

Diatonic Progressions

Now let's try putting chords together to create some progressions. These get progressively more difficult within each key.

Key of C

Key of F

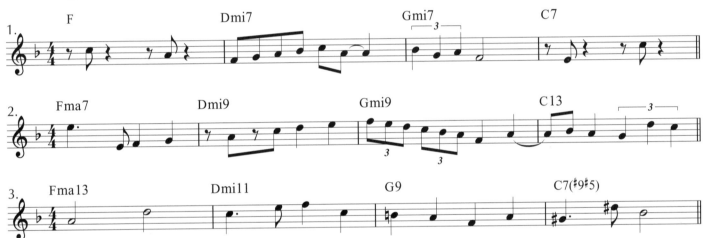

Key of G

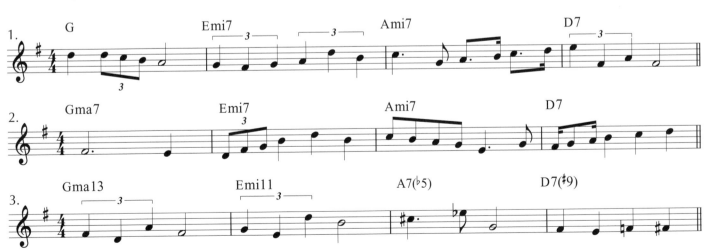

Chart Reading (Bass and Chords)

Here's something even more advanced: reading from a chord chart. Observe the chord symbols above each staff, and follow the rhythms indicated in the slash notation. Try each example twice:

- First, sing just the bass notes for each chord, in rhythm.
- Second, try "reading through" each chord, arpeggiating the chord tones (1-3-5-7). Also try singing 3rds and 5ths of different chords.

Duets

Sing these with a friend, or play the other part on piano. Be sure to try both parts. Transpose these if necessary to fit your vocal range.

Key of C

Key of F

Four-Part Harmony

This is another good way to practice "singing through chords." Find three other vocalists to sing with, or play the other parts on a piano.

C (1–3–5)

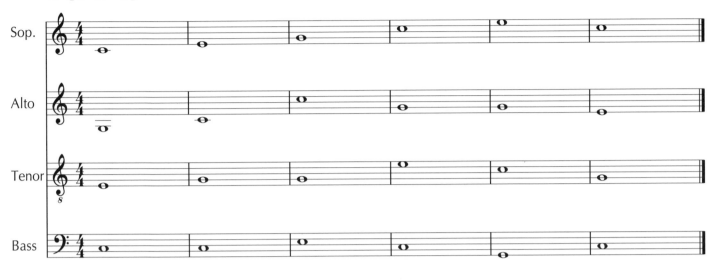

C6 (1–3–5–6)

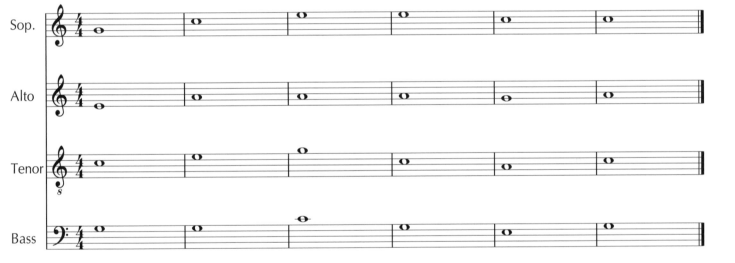

Cma7 (1–3–5–7)

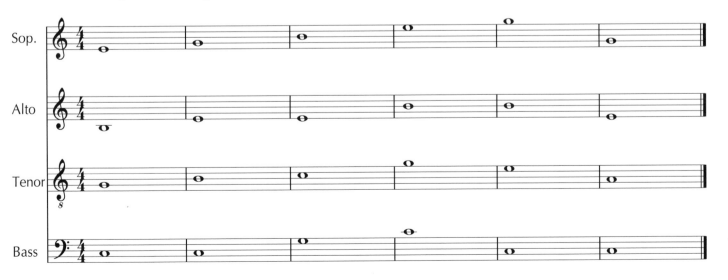

C7 (1–3–5–♭7)

C°7 (1–♭3–♭5–♭♭7)*

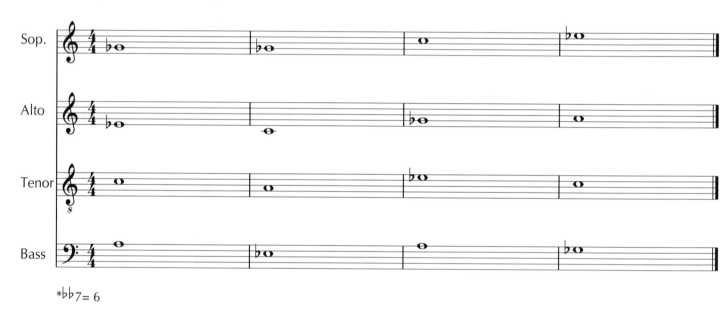

*♭♭7 = 6

C+ (1–3–♯5)

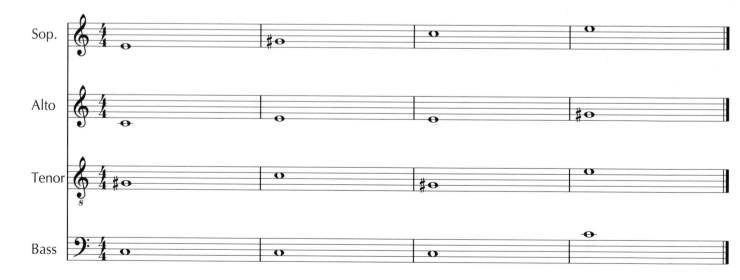

Cmi (1–♭3–5)

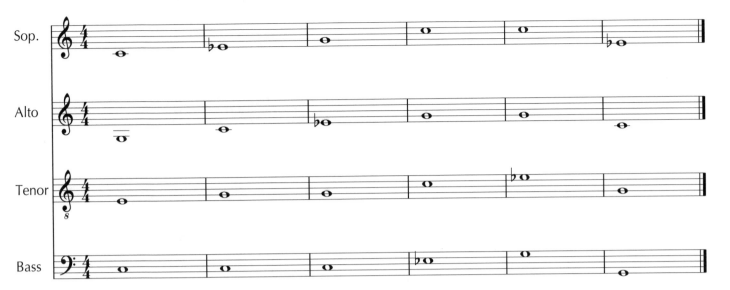

Cmi7 (1–♭3–5–♭7)

ABOUT THE AUTHORS

Mike Campbell has appeared in concerts and jazz festivals across the United States, Canada, Europe, and Australia. He has recorded seven solo albums and CDs and collaborated with the likes of Nancy Wilson, Dr. Donald Byrd, and Brazilian composer Moacir Santos. He is featured on the Herb Geller autobiographical CD *Playing Jazz.*

In his 35-year professional career, Mike has opened for or performed with a range of artists, including Ella Fitzgerald, Sarah Vaughn, Benny Carter, Count Basie, Henry Mancini, Petula Clark, Quincy Jones, The Supremes, The Mamas and the Papas, and many others. His voice has been heard in countless jingles, TV and movie soundtracks, and he has appeared on camera and sung on over forty television shows, including the *Ed Sullivan Show,* the *Roger Miller Show,* and others.

Mike has served on the Board of Governors of N.A.R.A.S. and is a member of A.S.C.A.P. He currently teaches at Musicians Institute in Hollywood and serves as the Vocal Program Director, and previously was Chairman of the vocal department at the renowned Grove School of Music. He has two instructional videos released by Warner Brothers and is the author of the book *Sightsinging: The Complete Method for Singers,* available from Hal Leonard Corporation.

A native of Los Angeles, Tracee Lewis Meyn wandered the hallowed halls of Musicians Institute for ten years—first as a student (earning VIT's Outstanding Student of the Year in '91) and then as an instructor—until the spring of '99, when fate took her to Oslo, Norway.

Tracee has sung for film and television in the U.S., toured in Europe as a blues singer, and sung or recorded with artists such as Steve Vai, Kenny Loggins, and Paul Anka. She is now working with various artists in Norway, recording a new CD with the Porters, due out in summer 2001, and working as a vocal instructor in the Oslo area.

Musicians Institute Press

is the official series of Southern California's renowned music school, Musicians Institute. **MI** instructors, some of the finest musicians in the world, share their vast knowledge and experience with you – no matter what your current level. For guitar, bass, drums, vocals, and keyboards, **MI Press** offers the finest music curriculum for higher learning through a variety of series:

ESSENTIAL CONCEPTS
Designed from MI core curriculum programs.

MASTER CLASS
Designed from MI elective courses.

PRIVATE LESSONS
Tackle a variety of topics "one-on-one" with MI faculty instructors.

BASS

rpeggios for Bass
Dave Keif • Private Lessons
695133 . . . . $12.95

he Art of Walking Bass
Bob Magnusson • Master Class
695168 Book/CD Pack $17.95

ass Fretboard Basics
Paul Farnen • Essential Concepts
695201 . . . . $14.95

ass Playing Techniques
Alexis Sklarevski • Essential Concepts
695207 . . . . $16.95

rooves for Electric Bass
David Keif • Private Lessons
695265 Book/CD Pack. $14.95

atin Bass
George Lopez and David Keif • Private Lessons
695543 Book/CD Pack. $14.95

Music Reading for Bass
Wendy Wrehovcsik • Essential Concepts
695203 . . . . $10.95

dd-Meter Bassics
Dino Monoxelos • Private Lessons
695170 Book/CD Pack. $14.95

GUITAR

dvanced Guitar Soloing
Daniel Gilbert & Beth Marlis • Essential Concepts
695636 Book/CD Pack. $19.95

dvanced Scale Concepts
Licks for Guitar
Jean Marc Belkadi • Private Lessons
695298 Book/CD Pack $14.95

asic Blues Guitar
Steve Trovato • Private Lessons
695180 Book/CD Pack $14.95

lues/Rock Soloing for Guitar
Robert Calva • Private Lessons
695680 Book/CD Pack $17.95

hord Progressions for Guitar
Tom Kolb • Private Lessons
695664 Book/CD Pack $14.95

lassical & Fingerstyle
Guitar Techniques
David Oakes • Master Class
695171 Book/CD Pack. $14.95

ontemporary Acoustic Guitar
Eric Paschal & Steve Trovato • Master Class
695320 Book/CD Pack. $16.95

reative Chord Shapes
Jamie Findlay • Private Lessons
695172 Book/CD Pack. $9.95

Diminished Scale for Guitar
by Jean Marc Belkadi • Private Lessons
00695227 Book/CD Pack. $9.95

Essential Rhythm Guitar
by Steve Trovato • Private Lessons
00695181 Book/CD Pack. $14.95

Funk Guitar
by Ross Bolton • Private Lessons
00695419 Book/CD Pack. $14.95

Guitar Basics
by Bruce Buckingham • Private Lessons
00695134 Book/CD Pack. $16.95

Guitar Fretboard Workbook
by Barrett Tagliarino • Essential Concepts
00695712 . . . . $14.95

Guitar Hanon
by Peter Deneff • Private Lessons
00695321 . . . . $9.95

Guitar Lick•tionary
by Dave Hill • Private Lessons
00695482 Book/CD Pack. $17.95

Guitar Soloing
by Dan Gilbert & Beth Marlis • Essential Concepts
00695190 Book/CD Pack. $19.95
00695638 VHS Video $19.95

Harmonics for Guitar
by Jamie Findlay • Private Lessons
00695169 Book/CD Pack. $9.95

Jazz Guitar Chord System
by Scott Henderson • Private Lessons
00695291 . . . . $9.95

Jazz Guitar Improvisation
by Sid Jacobs • Master Class
00695128 Book/CD Pack. $17.95
00695639 VHS Video $19.95

Jazz-Rock Triad Improvising
by Jean Marc Belkadi • Private Lessons
00695361 Book/CD Pack. $14.95

Latin Guitar
by Bruce Buckingham • Master Class
00695379 Book/CD Pack. $14.95

Modern Approach to Jazz,
Rock & Fusion Guitar
by Jean Marc Belkadi • Private Lessons
00695143 Book/CD Pack. $14.95

Modern Jazz Concepts for Guitar
by Sid Jacobs • Master Class
00695711 Book/CD Pack $16.95

Modern Rock Rhythm Guitar
by Danny Gill • Private Lessons
00695682 Book/CD Pack. $14.95

Modes for Guitar
by Tom Kolb • Private Lessons
00695555 Book/CD Pack. $16.95

Music Reading for Guitar
by David Oakes • Essential Concepts
00695192 . . . . $16.95

The Musician's Guide to Recording
Acoustic Guitar
by Dallan Beck • Private Lessons
00695505 Book/CD Pack. $12.95

The Musician's Guide to Recording
Drums
by Dallan Beck • Private Lessons
00695755 Book/CD Pack. $19.95

Outside Guitar Licks
by Jean Marc Belkadi • Private Lessons
00695697 Book/CD Pack. $14.95

Practice Trax for Guitar
by Danny Gill • Private Lessons
00695601 Book/CD Pack. $14.95

Progressive Tapping Licks
by Jean Marc Belkadi • Private Lessons
00695748 Book/CD Pack. $14.95

Rhythm Guitar
by Bruce Buckingham & Eric Paschal •
Essential Concepts
00695188 Book. $16.95
00695644 VHS Video $19.95

Rock Lead Basics
by Nick Nolan & Danny Gill • Master Class
00695144 Book/CD Pack. $15.95
00695637 VHS Video $19.95

Rock Lead Performance
by Nick Nolan & Danny Gill • Master Class
00695278 Book/CD Pack. $16.95

Rock Lead Techniques
by Nick Nolan & Danny Gill • Master Class
00695146 Book/CD Pack. $15.95

Slap & Pop Technique for Guitar
00695645 Book/CD Pack. $12.95

Texas Blues Guitar
by Robert Calva • Private Lessons
00695340 Book/CD Pack. $16.95

FOR MORE INFORMATION, SEE YOUR LOCAL MUSIC DEALER,
OR WRITE TO:

HAL•LEONARD®
CORPORATION

7777 W. BLUEMOUND RD. P.O. BOX 13819 MILWAUKEE, WI 53213

Visit Hal Leonard Online at **www.halleonard.com**

Prices, contents, and availability subject to change without notice

0604